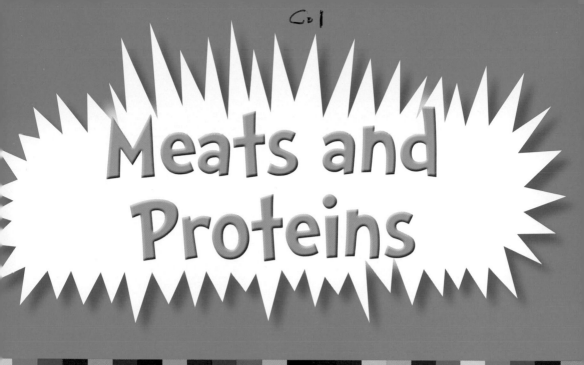

Meats and Proteins

BY ALLISON LASSIEUR

amicus
high interest

Amicus High Interest is an imprint of Amicus
P.O. Box 1329, Mankato, MN 56002
www.amicuspublishing.us

Library of Congress Cataloging-in-Publication Data
Lassieur, Allison, author.
 Meats and proteins / by Allison Lassieur.
    pages cm. — (Where does our food come from?)
 Summary: "Describes meats and proteins, an essential part of a
healthy diet, including both plant and animal sources of protein,
why they are healthy for us, and how other parts of the world
consume meat and protein foods"— Provided by publisher.
 Audience: K to grade 3.
 Includes bibliographical references and index.
 ISBN 978-1-60753-498-3 (library binding) —
 ISBN 978-1-60753-705-2 (ebook)
 1. Meat—Juvenile literature. 2. Proteins—Juvenile literature. I.
Title.
 TX373.L27 2015
 664.9—dc23
                                          2013035393

Editors: Rebecca Glaser and Tram Bui
Series Designer: Kathleen Petelinsek
Book Designer: Heather Dreisbach
Photo Researcher: Kurtis Kinneman

Photo Credits: Roxana Bashyrova/Shutterstock, cover (top);
Baishev/Shutterstock, cover (middle); nanantachoke/
Shutterstock, cover (bottom); Olga Nayashkova/Shutterstock,
5; Steve Bloom Images/Alamy, 6; natu/Shutterstock, 9;
Alexander Chaikin/Shutterstock, 10; Eugene Sergeev/
Shutterstock, 13; Be Good/Shutterstock, 14; FLPA/SuperStock,
17; lupu robert ciprian/Shutterstock, 18; Ton Koene/age
fotostock/SuperStock, 21; phototy/Shutterstock, 23; Blend
Images/Ronnie Kaufman/Larry Hirshowit/Getty Images, 25; D.
Hurst/Alamy, 27; ilolab/Shutterstock, 28

Printed in the United States of America at Corporate Graphics
in North Mankato, Minnesota.

10 9 8 7 6 5 4 3 2 1

Table of Contents

What Are Meats and Proteins?

Do you like to eat ham or chicken? Maybe you like bacon. All of these foods are meats. Meat comes from the **muscle** of animals. Beef is from cattle. **Poultry** comes from large birds. We eat chickens, turkeys, ducks, and geese. Ham and pork come from pigs. All of these meats are part of the meat and **protein** food group.

Sausage, eggs, and beans make a great meal. They are full of protein.

5

**Salmon is a kind of fish
that has lots of protein.**

 How much protein should you eat every day?

Protein is a **nutrient** that your body needs to grow. Your body uses up all its protein each day. So you need to eat some protein foods every day.

Meat is only one kind of protein food. Eggs, beans, and nuts have protein, too. So do fish and shellfish.

 Kids should eat 4 ounces of protein every day. One egg or a tuna sandwich counts as 1 ounce (28 g). A small hamburger counts as 2 to 3 ounces (56 to 84 g).

Some people don't eat meat. They are called **vegetarians**. But they still need protein. They get it from plant foods. Some kinds of beans and peas have about as much protein as meat. Soybeans, red beans, and black-eyed peas have lots of protein. Artichokes and spinach have it too.

 Which kind of bean has the most protein?

Soybeans are a good way to get protein if you don't eat meat.

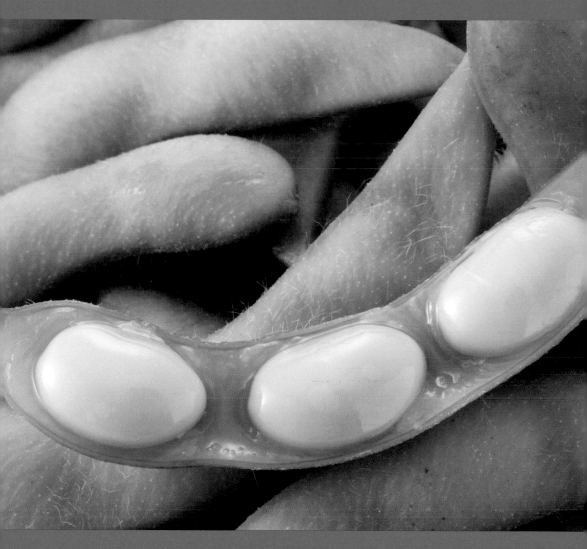

 Soybeans.

**Cattle live on farms.
Their meat is called beef.**

 How much meat do Americans eat every year?

How Do We Get Meats and Proteins?

Beef comes from cattle. They are raised on farms. Then they go to a packing plant. The animals are killed and cut into meat. Some of the beef goes to stores. The rest of the beef goes to **processing plants**. That beef is made into foods such as hot dogs, ground beef, and sausage. Some beef goes into canned food such as stews.

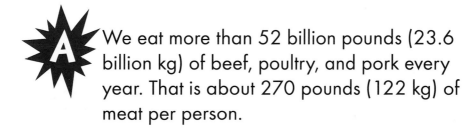 We eat more than 52 billion pounds (23.6 billion kg) of beef, poultry, and pork every year. That is about 270 pounds (122 kg) of meat per person.

Most fish and shellfish come from the ocean. Fishermen catch millions of fish. But that is not enough fish for everyone in the world to eat. So some seafood, such as shrimp, is raised on fish farms. Some fish farms grow salmon and catfish. The fish grow in huge tanks or cages.

 What seafood do Americans like best?

This fish farm is in the ocean. Fish are raised here.

A Shrimp. More people eat shrimp than any other seafood.

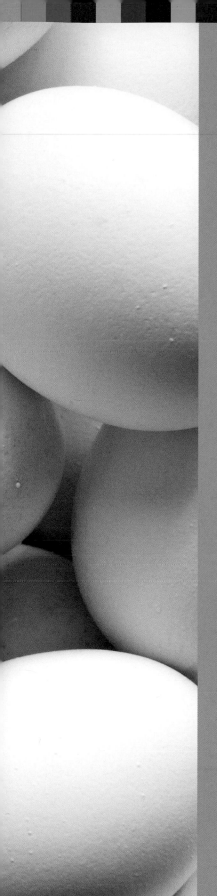

Eggs are packed with protein. Chickens lay billions of eggs every year. Most of those eggs go to a store. Others go to a food processing plant. Those eggs are used to make foods like bread and ice cream. Some stay on the farm. They hatch into chicks and grow up. Then the chickens lay more eggs!

Eggs have a lot of protein!

Where Is Meat Raised?

Most of the meat you eat comes from the United States. The U.S. grows more beef than anywhere else in the world. Beef cattle are raised mostly in the middle of the country, from Kansas down to Texas. Iowa is the top state for raising pigs. Most chickens are raised in the South.

 Do more people in the U.S. eat hamburgers or cheeseburgers?

We get both eggs and
meat from chickens.

 Cheeseburgers.

Shrimp and other seafood are healthy protein foods.

Almost all of the seafood we eat comes from other countries. But it spoils quickly. So how can we get seafood from far away? Freeze it! Frozen seafood will not spoil. It can be sent almost anywhere. This way, you can eat shrimp from Thailand or salmon from Canada.

Meat and Protein Around the World

Beef is easy to get in the U.S. It is not as easy to find in some places. Beef, pork, and goat are popular in Africa. But meat costs a lot there. Most African people only eat meat on special days. They get most of their protein from beans, vegetables, and nuts. People near the coasts or rivers eat a lot of fish.

Goats are a source of meat
for some people in Africa.

Would you eat a bug? Lots of people do! Some countries cannot grow protein foods. So they find other foods that have it. Insects have lots of protein. Beetles are popular to eat in African countries. People in Thailand love deep-fried grasshoppers, ants, worms, and bees. Yum!

 What's the most popular meat in the world?

Insects such as grasshoppers can be fried and eaten for protein.

 Pork!

Bacon and eggs can give you protein to start the day.

Healthy Meats and Proteins

Why is protein important? It helps to build your blood. Your muscles, bones, and skin need it. And it helps your hair and fingernails grow. Protein keeps your body healthy.

Meats have other nutrients, too. Meats have iron. Your blood needs iron to carry oxygen. **Omega-3s** are in fish and seafood. They help your heart and brain.

Meats are **complete proteins**. That means they have all the protein your body needs. Beans and nuts are **incomplete proteins**. They have only some of the protein you need.

To get enough protein, eat many kinds of foods. You could eat eggs for breakfast. Have beans for lunch and nuts for a snack. Eat a grilled chicken sandwich for dinner.

It is best to get protein from a variety of foods.

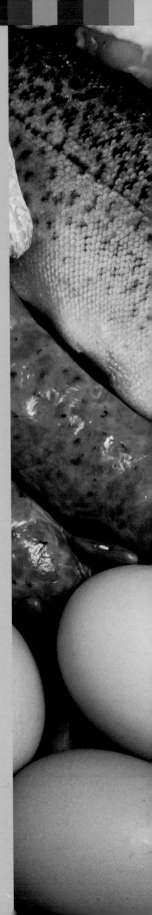

Beans are good to add in foods like tacos.

 Can you eat too much meat?

How much meat and protein should you eat? About one-fourth of your plate should have protein foods. Chicken, fish, and beans are good protein foods. They are also low-fat. What if you don't like beans? Hide them in other foods! Soups and chili have beans. Lots of Mexican foods have beans, too. Protein helps you stay healthy. Your body loves it.

 Yes. Most Americans already eat more red meat than they need. Put down that steak! Eat other kinds of protein, like red beans or tuna.

Glossary

complete protein A protein that has all the amino acids your body needs.

incomplete protein A protein that has only some of the amino acids your body needs.

muscle A part of the body that helps you move.

nutrient A chemical that is needed by people, animals, and plants to stay strong and healthy.

omega-3s Fatty acids found in fish and fish oil that have many health benefits.

poultry Birds such as chickens, turkeys, geese, and ducks, used as food.

processing plant A place that makes meat and other ingredients into foods sold to consumers.

protein An important nutrient found in some plants and animals.

vegetarian A person who does not eat meat.

Read More

Cleary, Brian P. *Black Beans and Lamb, Poached Eggs and Ham: What Is in the Meat and Beans Group?* Minneapolis: Millbrook Press, 2011.

Dickmann, Nancy. *Protein.* Chicago: Heinemann Library, 2012.

Lee, Sally. *The Powerful Protein Group.* Mankato, Minn.: Capstone Press, 2012.

Websites

Eating Well with Canada's Food Guide
www.hc-sc.gc.ca/fn-an/food-guide-aliment/index-eng.php

Kids' Fun Food Games
www.nourishinteractive.com/kids

KidsHealth: Learning About Proteins
kidshealth.org/kid/nutrition/food/protein.html

MyPlate Kids' Place
www.choosemyplate.gov/kids/index.html

Index

About the Author

Allison Lassieur tries to eat plenty of fresh, good foods at every meal. She has written more than 100 books for kids. Allison especially likes to write about history, food, and science. She lives in a house in the woods with her husband, daughter, three dogs, two cats, and a blue fish named Marmalade.